Not An Artist

Emily Philbrook

Dedicated to H & B & A & my ESP's, my angels, my best friends

These poems are for all of the people who think that artistry has been outdone. Who simply cannot fathom creating anything new. And these poems are for you, for your inner child, for your inner voices, for the sad days, and for the good days. For you, and you alone, and for them.

May God Be A Woman, A Giver
===========================

Fragile girl,

Run amongst the wildflowers
Through the meadows in the deep valley
Breathe the mountain air and drink the river water
Become one with Her, God, a She

Soft

You are reading aloud; I hear the inflections in your soft voice as the flow of the words drifts in and out. You pause, for just a moment, and as I peer up at you, I find your eyes glued to mine. You were watching to make sure I was listening.

Mild Love

I want you, to put it mildly. I want to wake you up with sleepy kisses trailing across your bare chest; I want the mornings in the shower as the water drips down your spine. Your hands buried in my hair; tongues entwined, our bodies nearly combusting with heat and passion and love, so much love.

<u>Untangle</u>

You told me you liked when my hair was tangled
Admired the mess and the curls and the unbrushed
Because it meant that I had slept a little later
Dreams lasting a little longer
And I had just this once
Cared a little less about what they thought
Well, of course, except
For you

New Mother

Take care of her
She's not as soft in the middle as me, more jaded and
scarred and cracked, less naive.
Take care of her because I worry that she feels alone
You were like a mother to me
Mother her
Like the way the willow trees used to hold my hopes and
dreams while I read Jane Austen in the late August sun
Please hold her like that
Take care of her while I am away
So that upon my return
I find her stronger than when I left
And you,
A new mother, born again.

<u>Freedom</u>

I saw you today. Not you in the droves of sunflowers. But you in the small patches of overgrown wildflowers that surrounded the festival. The unperturbed beauties that people don't pay to look at, often miss, but I notice with fervent eyes. You, all wilted and outgrown and tired. You, all uncontrolled and free. Free, that's it, you're free. Not like the rest of us. Not like the sunflowers.

Cigarette Light

I can see you beside me, calloused hand on my inner
thigh, thumbing little circles, absent-mindedly.

Absent-mindedly, like the way your hands find the way
to the small of my back in the rushed darkness.

Absent-mindedly like the way your knee grips the
steering wheel as you reach for the pack of Marlboros
that I tossed in the waste bin last night

Your shallow breaths beside me, my reminder
Those damn things will kill you,
Can't let you die first, I thought
Absent-mindedly

Wake Up

The patterned tapestries melt against the one small light that blinks every few seconds. The space is cramped, tucked neatly beneath the floorboards of this stolen home. I hear your soft breathing against my neck as the silk sheets we tore from the bed that doesn't belong to us rush between my legs. You trace my collarbone, tell me not to make a sound. We don't want to wake the neighbors, you say. But baby, we woke the whole world.

<u>Colors</u>

Paint me in the colors of your lips
Leave me dripping sunsets and roses

<u>Vanilla Love</u>

Cascading down the stairs in your t-shirt, I can see the shape of you illuminated by the refrigerator light, and as I wrap my arms around your waist, tasting the sweet vanilla on your lips, trailing kisses across your neck, I remember the reasons I fell for you.

<u>Mistakes</u>

I think about you at the most inopportune times
When I'm talking to my friends,
I wonder what you would say to us now
Would you give us words of wisdom
Or would you watch us stumble
Making our own mistakes
The way you did,
The way you still do

Burdens

Your hand is littered with scars of your past
The calloused skin, the worn knuckles, the cigarette
burns
Take my untouched hand in yours,
I want to carrie your burdens on the tips of my fingers

<u>Wild</u>

Love me wild; let me feel the demons roaring
inside your bones.

Gentle

Love me gently; soft and slow, I want to bathe in
the essence of you

<u>Snow Days</u>

Sticky hot chocolate breath
Upon reddened noses
Mittens made of pink and purple and yellow,
Holding tiny fingers to be kissed back to life
Snow dripping from frost-bitten toes
Soft voices asking for just five more minutes
These are the moments when I realize
All that She has given me

<u>New</u>

Stuck in that memory for the rest of my life
Replaying the way you brushed my hair behind my ear
The smirk growing across your stubble-laden cheeks
Leaning in,
So close, too close
I can still smell your aftershave
Hear your whisper
As I watch this memory become new
Over and over

<u>Sweet</u>

Trace the lines of my hip bone with your lips
Your tongue will know the taste of my skin like sugar,
Sweet, soft, slow
Like your hand in mine as we run across the sand
Plunging into the sea
Me in front of you
Looking back to the lines that paint your smile
That descend into me, beyond me, bliss

<u>Hey, Hannah</u>

You told me to be present. To listen. Han, I am listening.
I hear our laughter pitter-patter against the waves. I hear
saltwater taffy wrappers and playful slaps and my own
blissful, uncontrollable giggles. I hear God. I hear Her,
right here, right now. I hear Her in you. I hear her in
Bailey. And because of you, I hear Her within me

Done Playing The Game

Dad always tells me to play society's game
To conform, to do what I need to do to
Make it through this life unscathed
But I want to be scarred
I want live a life of constant ache
bleeding, bruised, burned
How dare I shy away from the pain
That you have built me to withstand

<u>My God, She Made You For Me</u>

It's summer now, the cicadas
Hum to the tune of the crickets and your breathing
And I lose myself as I watch you in the sunlit yard
Watering the marigolds and lilies
She made you for me
Made the soft curving of your spine
The arch of your shoulders
The strength of your arms
The beauty of your mind
It was Her who grew those flowers
So that I may have the privilege
Of watching them bloom

Present

You carry my heels
As I walk barefoot through the cobblestone streets
Drunk on cheap wine
The lights from nearby restaurants illuminating the alley
way
As I float across that little village
Where we had taken refuge
Away from the real world
You tell me to hurry along, but
I do not do as I am told
And so I linger just a moment longer
And soak up all that is and will be

<u>Butterfly Effect</u>

You matter. Even on your worst days. You have made an
impact on someone somewhere. Your presence matters.
Maybe it's that time you told that girl her hair was nice,
After her boyfriend had told her he hated it
Maybe it's that time you hugged that guy after he lost his
Mom, and now, he knows it's okay to cry
Maybe it's that dog you adopted from the shelter after
the hurricane, Scout's little paws need your hands.
You matter. You mean something to someone. I promise.

Discover Me

Explore me: travel to undiscovered places of my skin and make it known that you have visited.

<u>Carnivals</u>

When I asked you to take me out
I didn't mean here, too many people
Sure, the ocean touching the horizon as we reach the top
of the ferris wheel is beautiful
Sure, there is value in the smell of funnel cakes and
cotton candy
But I don't need all of this,
I need you,
And me,
And the never-ending sky
Clouds made of cotton candy rolling by

Rockabye

Lull me to sleep
The way you would a child
In a purple nightgown and wet hair
Soothe the hard-edged courses of my spine
Sing sweet songs as you hush
My only attempt to speak
Cradle me in your arms
With you,
I am small again

<u>Healer</u>

You promised to fix me
Make me all better
So that I could walk on my own again

So you fed me, watered me, sheltered me
Bathed me in the scent of you, showering in your love
And still

I couldn't do it on my own, never getting better now

Bill, What Did You Do?

There's a lovely photo of the two of you dancing. Hilary
is radiant, vibrant red lipstick against her pale skin,
smiling as you spin her around the White House
ballroom, seemingly unaware of the storm passing
through.

Say, Bill, I wonder if she knew then,
Knew about Paula, about Monica,
Knew about all of the other women

Tell me, Bill, was it worth it?
To ruin your career, to ruin your marriage, to ruin
Monica,
Riddle me this, would you do it again?

<u>Highway Motels</u>

The text said to meet you here
At the rundown motel beside the freeway
And as usual
I did as I was told
Even though the sheets were musty and clung to the
sweat on our skin, large stains from long cigarette drags
on the ceiling, the desperate need to shower away the
grime
I still let you take me there
And a part of me never left

<u>Pause</u>

Breathe in. You are here now. You are reading this page.
You have come this far and you can't quit now. Keep
going, breathing, existing, surviving.

<u>Yellow</u>

His running shoes were the kind you find at a
consignment shop
Worn, a dingy yellow, reminiscent of a wilting sunflower,
Falling over in exhaustion from holding the weight
Of its' very self
Much like his weakening calves
As the cancer struck his every muscle
Like the guitar he used to play her before she fell asleep
She would say
"Daddy, let me hear one more"
Except this time, he simply had no more left to give

Picture-Perfect

Even on my best nights,
I will never be worthy of a front cover
Drugstore lipstick, cheap liquor, years old mascara
Glasses uncleaned, nails bitten off, socks mismatched
Nothing about me will ever photogenic
But maybe,
I am meant to be written about
Not photographed

Hey, Bailey

It's late now, closing in on curfew
I am tired, feet blistering, as I slip off my heels
And I know you had a bad night,
Your grip on the steering wheel tight, jaw clenched
But you drive me home anyways,
Because I asked you
And even though it's dark,
I don't need to turn around to know
That you wait in the driveway
Until I am inside
Safe

<u>Satisfied</u>

Our eyes lock, only for a moment, but it is enough to make you stutter, your words tripping over one another, until I look down, satisfied with the effect I have on you, and with cheeks now flushed and palms sweating, you continue speaking, with a slight shake in your voice, until you hit your pace once again. It is in these moments in which I love you the most.

Soft Love

Lay me down softly; letting my hair fall around me as you gently remove the barriers between us. We will become one.

<u>Someday</u>

My child,
You are not here yet. You might never be.
But if She chooses to bless this Earth
With your presence, may you know,
You were born with a different fire than the rest
And although you may burn,
You will also ignite
Live for that

<u>Do Good</u>

Watch the news
Get involved
Care about the people around you

Tell a stranger something kind
Raise awareness where you see injustice
Be a good human being

-all that I ask from my students

<u>Drunk</u>

The floor is sticky here
Frat house bathrooms are moldy and covered in god knows
what
But I am too weak to stand as I lie
With my face to the cool tile, afraid to lift my head
For fear more bile will rise from my throat
I shouldn't have come here
But I didn't know what to do
When I drink
I come alive

<u>Nah.</u>

How funny, I fell in love with another poet
           if sex is poetry in motion
Are all boys poets?

Mind-Reader

Press your palm to my temple, feel my soul
-deeper than most

Dear Mommy, Love Emily

There will come a day when my mother will no longer be here to soothe away my nightmares or butterfly kiss the pain away. There will come a time when I will have to learn to take care of myself on my own. And when that day comes, I will do it all the same. Because my mother taught me the best.

<u>Pure</u>

Under the magnolias,
The Louisiana sun kissed us farewell
As the fireflies came out for a dance,
Begging us to supply the music, our laughter
Beside each other in the overgrown grass
Hands intertwined, this must be
What Heaven feels like

Writer's Fallacy

In an effort to put me in my place
A girl once told me
There is nothing special about writing
Everyone can do that

The problem is,
Not everyone can write from your individual perspective
New styles, unique looks on the world, on literature
There is nothing easy about writing
But there is something so invariably brave

<u>Last Chance</u>

I asked you to meet me here
To tell you goodbye
Because when you wake up tomorrow
I'll be in a new city
Tranquil and far away
New taxis to chase, lights to admire
And you'll still be here
Stagnant, unwavering,
I promise I am going to get on that place
And never look back

Virtual Reality

It's a lot easier to sound brave
On a tiny little screen
Micro-pixels of courage
That disappear with one click of your finger

It's a lot easier forget your problems
When you can unplug from the source

You can't see of the things they are saying
About you, about him, about what they think
They know about what you had

It all goes away
Just like… that

<u>Good Riddance</u>

I am not going to apologize for unfollowing you in real life

        - I don't owe anyone justification

Dark Academia Meets Frat Parties
=====

Everybody assumes that poets spend their time
In libraries and dainty coffee shops
Sipping on malted lattes and reading Hemingway

But what about the poets
Who spend their time in nightclubs and dive bars
Drowning in vodka and whiskey and electronic music

Aren't those the poets who have a little more to say
About the true human experience
In all of its' grit and glory

Questions For You

I have asked for an answer so many times
Why did you choose me

Was I different than all the other girls
Or was I just the only one who cared enough to ask
If you were okay

How dare you say that I am crazy
When I am the only one who stood by your side
And convinced them that you weren't

<u>Dying Thoughts</u>

I wonder where you are now
Probably on the sand, toes being buried by little fingers
Baby A's tiny pink tankini muddied by the sea
And the sand the tide has left to drown

I bet your wife has packed a picnic lunch
Sandwiches cut into triangles
Just the way you like
And lemonade with a sweet aftertaste

She wants to build a castle now
And you follow her lead
Fetching buckets of water, moats, tunnels
Anything for her, my sweet child

I gave her to you as a gift
My last wish to see you as a father
And although I couldn't be a mother
I trusted you to find one, good enough for her

<u>You Are More</u>

You're not a distraction. You're not a side chick. You're not a home wrecker. You're not a slut.

You're a girl who fell in love with someone who didn't love her back.

You're so much more.

<u>Hey, Ana</u>

Mint gum, cold limbs
Too large sweaters, herbal tea
Bathroom trips, bottles of water
Ignoring the hunger cues, crying
Lots of crying
         -if you can understand this, start recovery, please

<u>Anywhere, But Here</u>

Run away to Italy with me
Let's get lost in the cobblestone alleyways
Kiss me against the wall of a corner shop
Buy me a bouquet from the market
Dance to the music of the street musicians
We are going to the live life you always promised

<u>Gone</u>

The first thing you said to me
After months of not speaking,
Let's get this goodbye over with

As if my tears were a burden for you
You let me touch you
But that was just it

You received me,
Gave nothing in return,
But a cold, forced embrace

And that's when I realize
It was really over
Maybe not for me,
But you didn't love me anymore

Unforgettable Moments

I peer over my desk to see you looking at me already and I raise my eyebrow. You're supposed to be working on that lesson plan and I am so supposed to be reading an article from the New Yorker. I can't focus on the words of some 20-something new writer when I have this moment to be looking at you. You haven't shaved in weeks and the stubble has started to grow on me, but I won't tell you that. You smirk and continue typing, but I know your chair is at just the right height to watch me over the top of your laptop. I let out my breath and return to reading, letting my hair fall loose, smiling an all-knowing glow.

<u>Drowning</u>

I wanted to drown in you; I was handed a lifejacket
instead.

        -being too deep always scared you

Hey, Addie

I know this life hasn't been fair to you
But I see so much in you

I see the way you protect those you love
Including me, with all that you have

The willingness to take the kind of risks you don't regret
Your strength despite all the woes thrown your way

You have given me so much, beautiful girl
And I just know

This life is going to give you back all that you have given
And when that day comes, I can say, I told you so

<u>Cherry</u>

She wore cherry chapstick that day. The day you decided that you had enough of this waiting game. It was February 3rd, two weeks before her brother's seventh birthday, three months since you had started dating. She had been wearing shorter skirts lately, even in the cold, and wanted you to kiss all of her worries away.

It was getting dark and the hot chocolate you had bought for her had grown cold. It was time for you to show her what you needed. You started to kiss her, but she broke away to say,
I need to be home before curfew

But she never made it home on time. Because you held her down, you didn't listen to her screams or her begging you to stop or her tears. You took what you wanted from her and made her walk home, her cherry chapstick smeared across her swollen lips, the same color as the blood running down her torn skirt.

<u>Home</u>

Build me our dream house
Not the kind in the magazines
Or those over-done reality shows

Build me a home with rooms for our children
For those who are bound to us by blood
And for the those with whom we simply share love

Build me a home with a nook for my reading
Where I may watch the snow fall
To the tune of Whitman's words

Build me a home with a willow tree in the yard
So that you and I may lay beneath the branches
And remember the sweetness of our love

<u>Never Enough</u>

I love you.
You made sure you said those words.
Because you couldn't be in love with me

Not while you were married to her
You loved me enough to dance with me
To dream of me
To write about me

But never enough to date me
To kiss me
To be in love with me

You did care
Just not enough

<u>Hate These Parties</u>

The room is full of people. Celebrating, congratulating, and we all take our seats. I don't look behind me to know your eyes are boring into the back of my head, and the speaker begins to talk and I turn around. Our eyes meet and the tension is the kind you feel deep in your chest. My palms begin to sweat and I pray for all of the hands I have to shake tonight. Why did you come here?

<u>Old Friends</u>

I knock on the door softly, afraid to startle you,
I didn't come here to be a distraction
The door is glass and for once I am grateful
As the look of shock turns into a smile
And you welcome me in

Aware of all the stares
I turn my back slightly, afraid to see their faces
But you remind me they are only children
And introduce me as an old friend

I blush and wave, but I can already hear the whispers
The siblings of those who came before
They know who I am
And why I came

Funny how you can travel the whole world
Grow and explore and become new
And still be made to feel
So incredibly small

Like The First Time

64

My first day back in town, I went to see you. Our parting words had left my heart aching, but I hoped that time would have healed the broken parts of us. I tell you to meet me here, at the run-down diner, and I order myself an old favorite, a strawberry milkshake, to pass the time. You walk through the door and the first thing I notice is you're not wearing your wedding ring. I make a point to ask. Sliding into the booth, you laugh. It's the same soft sound I remember and instantly, I am that girl again, falling for you. I ask about your ring. You say it's over. It takes until my milkshake is nearly gone for you to ask me on our first date.

<u>Valid</u>

It is okay to have an abortion just because you want one
                -stop making women ashamed of their rights

<u>Fires</u>

My Dad believes in souls, he says, because I was born with a fire in me. Because he, nor my mother, could have ever created whatever driving force is held within my heart without the help of God.

I have been afraid of my fire for so long, but Dad, here I am embracing it. Fueling it.

Remind Me Again Why I Teach

I watched that little boy struggle to find the words
To tell the pretty girl just how he felt
I said to him
Sweet boy, no need to rehearse
When the time is right,
The words will come
And so they did
Her little toothy smile perked up as he gave her
The little marigolds I helped him pick
From our class garden
And said
You shine like the flowers
In Miss. Emily's garden

<u>All I Ask</u>

Be the lover who searches all of the galaxies and nebulas until you find a star worthy of bringing to my palm for safe-keeping

<u>M.I.A.</u>

It's been a long while since anyone has heard news
They call it Missing in Action
But she knows in her heart
You are gone

They found your tags
Which she clutches every Sunday with her rosary beads
Praying to a God that she doesn't believe exists
That someday she will find peace

<u>False Narratives</u>

They told him his Daddy was a bad guy
That because he wore something different on his head
He is a part of something evil

They told him because he doesn't speak English well
He is not American, foreign, alien, except
He was born right here in New York

They told him his religion
Is villainous, full of terrorists,
Just like all the people on TV

They told him he was different
And to a child, different is bad
So he must be bad

This is what your prejudices teach a child
Think before you share that post on Facebook
Because you never know who might see it

<u>Little Things</u>

You round the corner and I notice two cups of coffee
instantly. You don't befriend your coworkers and you
have never had more than one black coffee in the three
years I have known you.

This one's for you, Em.
You say as place the cup in mine, still warm

I sip and taste the vanilla, the cream, and the sugar
You remembered
I graze your arm and you turn your head
I stop walking, you do too

I knew people were staring now
I say it loud and clear anyways

Thank you

Playing The Victim

72

You wonder why I can't let you all go
But I see your faces in my nightmares

The laughter and the gossip and the rumors
They haunt me

You don't get to torment people
And walk away untouched

You don't get to destroy someone
And leave unscathed

You hurt me. And you hurt him.
And I let you.

I was weak then,
But the tide is finally turning

And I may not win, but
Promise you, Karma always does

<u>For You</u>

I will love you until the day I die
            -you know who you are

<u>Mama</u>

My mother, in all her glory, is Jesus. She is kind and strong and patient.

Selfless and unwavering, a woman who lives to give herself to others.

My savior, healing wounds and erasing demons and giving grace

Bathe me in holy water, Mama, cleanse me of my sins,
Until I am born again

Right. Here.

I ask you to slow up as I pause to inhale. The fall air is crisp against my tired lungs. We have run three miles deep already into the expansive forest and I see a view spot up ahead. We sit, collecting our thoughts, and I rest my head on your shoulder. My once tight braids have fallen loose and I can already feel the sweat pooling in beads on my forehead. You slip your arm around me anyways, and as we look out across the foliage, I allow myself to exhale this breath I have been holding for months.

If all you did today was exist, I am proud of you.

Real Kindness

When I say "Be Kind"
That doesn't mean to stay silent against injustice
When I say "Be Kind"
That doesn't mean to stop standing up for yourself

Be kind to that stranger who is having a bad day
Be kind to nature as you move throughout your day

Be conscious of your words, your actions, your thoughts
But do not become complacent
Under the premise of
Being "kind"

<u>Empath</u>

A great man (well, maybe not so great) wrote once about
the true freedom of man being in caring about other
people, and you said, that is why you are free, Emily

For so long, caring burdened me
Too deeply, too much, too soon
I couldn't let go of those I love

I felt their pain in my bones, ached with their losses
Celebrated in their greatest triumphs
But I was so afraid of losing them

I didn't tell them how much I cared
Never telling you that I would let every piece of me die
Even this one

If it meant that you could live the rest of your life
In a relative sense of peace, so maybe this isn't freedom
Maybe this is chosen entrapment, my last act

Manipulation

It's funny how they really think you manipulated me.
You took advantage of a weak girl.

No, no, silly kids,
I had all the power

My energy controlled our actions
If I had wanted it to stop

It would have
Don't speak on what you don't know

<u>Daddy's Girl</u>

He used to sing his daughter the words of a rockstar.
Didn't grow up with lullabies or storybooks
Just Bon Jovi and Queen to get him through
And she grew up
To fall in love with those bands,
Sleeping in her dad's old tour T-shirts
That still fell to her knees even at 32
And when heard the first guitar strike
On that old cassette tape from her bedroom radio
She would let the sweet rock take her to sleep
Where she could finally see her Dad again
Only in her dreams

<u>Leaving Tomorrow</u>

It has grown dark now as our walk comes to a close and we rest on the front stoop. I leave in a month and we talk of shopping trips and errands and the monotonous routines of moving out of my childhood home. I look into your brown eyes, illuminated by the orange street light, and I see myself. For a brief moment. I am you. I am seeing my daughter leave for college. Seeing my world changing, uncertainty and doubt and fear, and I see you, Mom, for all that you are.

Moving On

I loved you. Past tense.

<u>Alive</u>

I used to write on little post-it notes and leave them scattered around your room for you to find. Some had jokes, questions, compliments, anything to make the dull void awaken something in you. I had seen glimpses of your aliveness, but never lasting more than a fleeting moment and I was determined to make those last.

When it ended, I knew there were still a few unfound, but I hope now, on your bad days, you can discover the good part of you again. The pieces of you that awakened something in me.

<u>Hey, Lizzy</u>

You're braiding my hair
The way you have since we were little girls
Racing to head wherever was next

The music is soft and background noise
To our laughter
I have missed you, my little sister

Missed the way you carry the weight of those
You love on your shoulders effortlessly
Missed your kindness, sincerity

Don't ever lose the part of you that is
So rare I have yet to find it in another
You're my four-leaf clover

Read To Me Again

If I could have stayed in that moment forever,
I would still

You, across the room, reading aloud to me,
An article about frankly, I didn't care what

Because your voice was heavenly, drifting around
The room like the pink clouds of a sunset

And I saw in awe
Of the God that sat in front of me

<u>I Tried</u>

It's Sunday morning and the chocolate chip pancakes I promised to serve you in bed are burning as I attempt to butter the toast, pour the orange juice, and turn off the stove.

I am too late and one side of the pancake is a charred black unrecognizable blob. I bring them to you anyways and you just smile, brush my frizzed hair behind my hair, and say thank you baby.

For you know, I was never a chef, in fact, I was never even a multitasker. You married me for my unkempt ways and my thoughtful quirks, thank you baby.

<u>Danger</u>

She knew he was drunk, the slurred words and the sway
Of his walk, she could smell the whiskey spewing from
His open pores, but she let him drive anyways
For fear of making a scene in front of the crowd outside
But now he was swerving between the yellow and she
Had to yank the steering wheel twice already
As he laughed and said how stupid she was

Stop the car, she screamed, and as he slammed the brakes
She opened the door and ran
Not coming back when he called her name

They found him in a ditch just a few blocks away
Struck a tree at 60 miles per hour, severe brain damage
The papers reported that if there had been a passenger
They would have been killed instantly

Anyone with any information was urged to come
forward, she never did.

Natural

You don't have to always be who they want you to be
-authenticity is valued

<u>Stop Pretending You Don't Care</u>

You told me there were no hard feelings
What the hell is that supposed to mean

I have hard feelings
You hurt me, you broke me, you decided I wasn't enough

Of course you can move on,
You didn't lose the person that you love

<u>Reality</u>

The lights float in and out of her vision, the too bright reds and blues and greens painting the faces of the strangers in the worn-down club as creatures of the night. High on Xanax, vodka, and sex, she's floating between the arms of men she doesn't know and the bartender, her feet swollen from dancing in the heels she outgrew years ago. Life isn't always some goddamn indie movie where the girls live dainty lives free of scandal, drinking lattes in sweaters. Her life was gritty and filled with scars and mistakes and tripping out and coming down, imperfect, real.

Vibrations

My energy is drawn to your light

Baby Sister, I Love You

Soft, tiny hands wrapped around my finger
Free of scars, new, untouched
Thin blonde hair that is messy from restful sleep
Eyelashes that tickle my elbow as we lay curled on our
sectional, me and Ella, the littlest thing
I have ever loved
In this moment,
It is just us, and I can feel all of the love I have for
This child, all my wishes for her future,
That she may know she is worthy, that she will know
She is enough and important
That her big sister will always be here
And love her more than even poetry could explain

No More Feeling

I feel everything and nothing all once
Everything makes my bones ache and collapses to the
deepest pit of my stomach, dissolving itself,
Extending, weaving through my rib cage,
hollow, empty
Yet full,
Everything and nothing

<u>If Your Serotonin Levels Need A Boost</u>

Pick me up at 8
Let's drive into the summer sunset, across the freeway
Blasting Y2K hits, screaming at the world
For what it has put us through
Reminding ourselves what it feels like
To live

Soundtrack To Our Lives

Merely background music to their wedding dance, the
song flows to the speed of the heels on my mothers feet,
guiding my father around the room. A moment in time
captured on video that I re-watch over and over again.
Not because of my mother's contagious laughter as my
Dad cracks yet another one of his jokes. Their newly-
minted rings upon their fingers touch, their hands
clasped together, his on top of hers, forever kind of love

<u>Take Me Back</u>

I would sell my soul to feel the joy I felt with you again

<u>Always, His</u>

His cold hands draw a shiver down my spine as he traces
the necklace across my collarbone, gently lifting the
jewelry to place a kiss beneath the space that it had
occupied, and for a moment, I let him. His lips feel
proper in their place on my skin and I start to disintegrate
beneath his touch as his arms wrap around my waist, I
am his again

<u>Love Letter To Myself</u>

I vow, to you, that I will never stop writing

<u>H&B&A: All My Love</u>

And to the best friends I've ever had
In this lifetime
I am saying to you
Thank you for giving me everything
There will never come a day where I am not
Thinking of you
And whether the sun sets in Rhode Island
or Seattle or New Hampshire
I am here
Saying to you that there will never be a sunset
Where I am not caring about you
Your hopes and dreams and fears
You are
The best things that have ever happened to me

You have reached the end of this piece of art. Keep writing. Keep creating. Keep caring. Keep loving.

Love is the truest form of art.

Be an artist everyday.

All my love,

(e.p.)

* 9 7 9 8 6 7 5 8 8 0 9 9 7 *